ACKNOWLEDGEMENT

I Would Like To Acknowledge

The CREATOR OF HEAVEN AND EARTH (GOD)
FOR ALL THAT HE HAS Given Me.
Thanking God I Am
For My Talents and Gifts.
I Recognize That The Lord Gave Me This Gift,
Which Allows Me To Share With Children And Everyone That Participates In The Reading Of The Literary Material That I Produce Through The Commission Of God.

Thank You Lord God

I Will Forever Be Grateful
For Your Trust In Me

Pamela Denise Brown

Copyright © 2019 Pamela Denise Brown
All rights reserved. No part of this book may be used or reproduced by any means, graphic, electronic, or mechanical, including photocopying, recording, taping or by any information storage retrieval system without the written permission of the publisher except in the case of brief quotations embodied in critical articles and reviews.

Books Speak For You books may be ordered through Amazon, booksellers or by contacting:
Books Speak For You At
Booksspeakforyou.com
OR
Booksspeakforyou@yahoo.com
The views expressed in this work are solely those of the author.
Any illustration provided by iStock and such images are being used for illustrative purposes.
Certain stock imagery © iStock.
ISBN: 978-1-64050-372-4
Library of Congress Control Number: 2019
Printed in the United States Of America

DEDICATION

I Dedicate This Book To My Amazing Mother, Queen Ella Brown, My Father Who Has Passed, Jesse Porter Brown, My Brother Who Recently Passed On March 24, 2019, Jesse Perry Brown, My Sister Casetta Josette Brown, My Three Children Carrayah Queen-Ella Coleman, Gabriel Joel Coleman, Carrynn Erin-Josette Coleman, My Great Nephews Isaiah Brown And Zaden Brown, My Four Best Friends, Tonya Brantley, Monica Lee, Robbynn Johnson And Jacqui Frazier-Lyde, My Special Cousin Sheranda (Sandy) Myers, My Friend In Christ, Angela Malson, AND Every Child Around The World That Has Ever Felt Alone, Abandoned, Misunderstood, Weird And Different... I DEDICATE This Book To You With Love!!

Pamela Denise Brown

DESCRIPTION

Save My Life Is A Reading Work Book, That Has A Panic Save My Life Sheet For Children To Turn Into Their Teacher, Counselor, Principal, Friend, Parent Or Neighbor... The Book Expresses The Feelings Of A Child About The Pain And Abandonment They Feel Emotionally Growing Up... The Book Is About Children Literally Asking Everyone Around Them For Help... Save My Life Is An Emotional Expression From A Child Whose Voice Is Sometimes Diminished... The Book Expresses The Pain Children Sometimes Feel When They're Alone, When They Feel Different And When They're Trying To Find Themselves... The Workbook Section Gives Children An Opportunity To Deal With Their Different Emotions Through Defined Words... There Is Also Room In The Book For Children To Journal Their Emotional Journey And Progression... This Is A Book That Will Allow Parents To Participate In The Discovery Of Their Child... I Suggest That The Child Read The Book And Do The Exercises And Then Give It To Their Parents And Teacher So They Can Have A Broader Scope Of The Child's Emotional State Without The Child Being Overexposed...

READS

Acknowledgement...2
Dedication...4
Description 5
Save My Life Read 7
Understanding Your Feelings...22
Workbook Section-Identify Your Feelings...35
Identify Who You Are With A List Of Positive Affirmations...40
Create Your Own Affirmations...44
30 Day Journey Journal...62
PANIC - Save My Life Panic Report Sheets...122
Save My Life Suspicion Sheet...129
Share Your Experiences...130
My Thank You Letter From President Obama, For My Tireless Efforts To Lift Up The Next Generation Of Thinkers, Dreamers And Doers...131
School Book Giveaway Sponsors...132
Thank You For Your Purchase...133
My Contact Information...134
Special Dedication To Children Around The World...135
Another Special Dedication To Children In Cities In The United States...141

SAVE MY LIFE

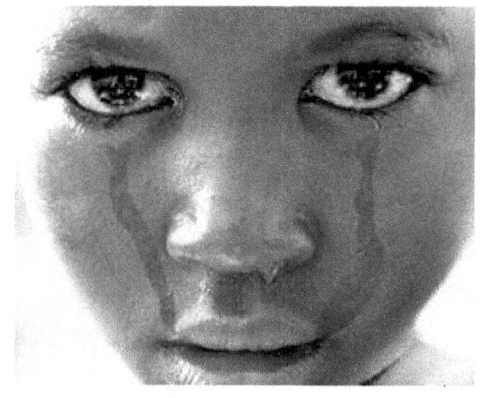

Save My Life...
Listen To Me...
I Have Something To Say...

Talk To Me...
I Need To Know You Care...
I'm Going Crazy Inside...
I Don't Know How I Feel...
I Don't Know What To Do...

Please As Much As You Can...
Tell Me You Love Me...
I Want To Be Loved...
I Want To Be Understood...
Have Patience With Me...
I'm Trying To Work Out My Life...
Take A Day Off And Spend It With Me...
Get To Know Who I'm Becoming...

Sometimes I Think About Killing Myself... But If You Spoke To Me And Perhaps Put Your Phone Down, You Would See, Just How Alone I Feel...

I'm Losing My Mind...
I Don't Know How To Pick Friends...
You Didn't Teach Me That...
I Don't Know How To Express Myself...
You Didn't Teach Me That...
I Feel Ignored And Alone...

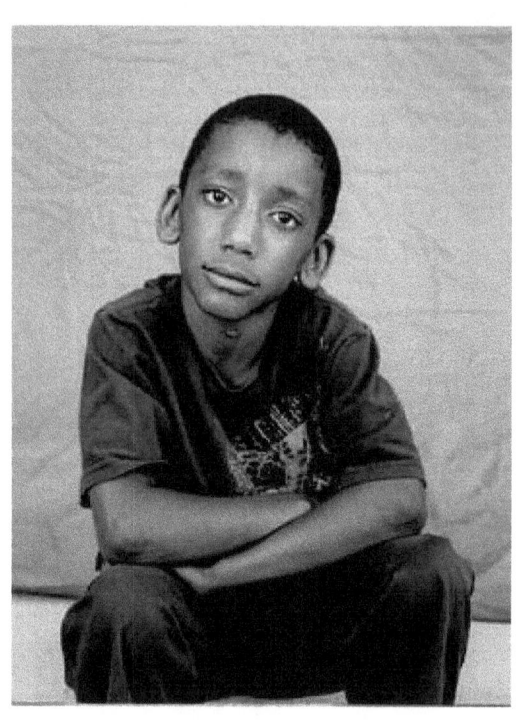

Why Should I Have To Figure This Out On My Own...
You Say When I Get 18, I Have To Move Out...
Where Am I Going???
I'm Still A Kid, 5+5+5+3, Now Why Would You Abandon Me...
Save My Life...

Teach Me What School Doesn't...
Spend Time With Me...
Listen To Me When I Talk...
I Need You...
I Love You, But I Don't Feel Like You Love Me...

Save My Life...
Inspire Me...
Encourage Me...
Give Me Hope...
Correct Me When I'm Wrong...
Be An Example For Me...
Learn How To Handle Me...
Fight Life With Me...
Fight Me With Me...
Save My Life...

I'm All Alone...
You Don't Know How To Approach Me...
You Don't Understand Me...
Look At Me...
See Me...
Talk To Me...
Save My Life...

I'm Confused...
What Do You Know About Confusion???
I Don't Know Why I Think The Way I Do...
I Don't Know Why I Act The Way I Act...
Reach Me...
Teach Me...
Listen To Me...
Hold Me...
Find A Resolution With Me...
Pray With Me...
Save My Life...

I Don't Want To Be This Way...
I Don't Know Who I Am...
I Don't Want To Hurt Anybody...
I Don't Want To Hurt Me...
Save My Life...

I'm Weird...
I'm Different...
Sometimes I Feel Out Of Place...
Out Of Line...
I Want To Be Able To Be Myself...
I Want To Be Able To Be Different...
I Want To Explore Who I Am...
If I Scream, I Want It To Be Ok...
I Need A Breakthrough To Get To Who I Am...
There's Someone In Me Fighting To Get Out...
Fighting To Be Heard...
Fighting To Be Understood...
Fighting To Be Unconditionally Loved...
Fighting To Be Myself...
Fighting To Know Who I Am...
Save My Life...

Let's Talk About Me...
Ask Me Some Questions...
Please Help Me...
Think About Me...
Help Me Reach Me...
Spend Some Time With Me...
Save My Life...

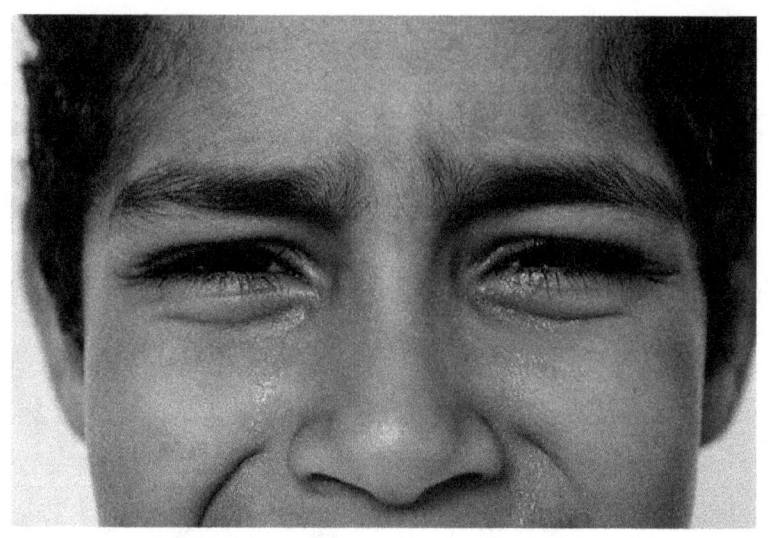

Help Me Fight The Fear...
Help Me Understand The Voices I Hear...
Accept That I'm Weird...
Make Me Feel Comfortable About Being Myself...
Help Me Develop My Best Possible Self...

SAVE MY LIFE!!!

UNDERSTANDING YOUR FEELINGS

Have You Ever Said Anything That You Just Read???
Below Is A List Of Feelings Use The Space Below And Define Them As Your Own Feelings Based On What They Mean To You

When You're Angry, You Can Feel

Annoyed_____
_____
_____

Workuped_____
_____
_____

Inflamed_____
_____
_____

Unpleasant_____
_____
_____

Hateful_____
_____
_____

Irritated_____
_____
_____

Hostile_____
_____
_____

Insulting_____
_____
_____

Sore_____

_____
_____
_____

Offensive_____

_____
_____
_____

Bitter_____

_____
_____
_____

Aggressive_____

_____
_____
_____

Infuriated_____

_____
_____
_____

When You're Helpless, You Can Feel

Alone_____
_____
_____
_____

Paralyzed_____
_____
_____
_____

Vulnerable_____
_____
_____
_____

Dominated_____
_____
_____
_____

Incapable_____
_____
_____
_____

Empty_____
_____
_____
_____

When You're Sad, You Can Feel

Sorrowful_____
_____
_____
_____

Unhappy_____
_____
_____
_____

Grief_____
_____
_____
_____

Dismayed_____
_____
_____
_____

When You're Hurt, You Can Feel

Wrong_____
_____
_____
_____

Alienated_____
_____
_____
_____

Heartbroken_____
_____
_____
_____

Victimized_____
_____
_____
_____

Offended_____
_____
_____
_____

When You're Depressed, You Can Feel

Powerless_____
_____
_____
_____

Discouraged_____
_____
_____
_____

Miserable_____
_____
_____
_____

Disappointed_____
_____
_____
_____

Guilty_____
_____
_____
_____

A Sense Of
Loss_____
_____
_____
_____

When You're Confused, You Can Feel

Uncertain_____
_____
_____
_____

Perplexed_____
_____
_____
_____

Skeptical_____
_____
_____
_____

Uneasy_____
_____
_____
_____

Unsure_____
_____
_____
_____

When You're Afraid, You Can Feel

Timid_____
_____
_____
_____

Fearful_____
_____
_____
_____

Anxious_____
_____
_____
_____

Humiliated_____
_____
_____
_____

Threatened_____
_____
_____
_____

When You're Indifferent, You Can Feel

Pre-
occupied_____
_____
_____
_____

Nonchalant_____
_____
_____
_____

Reserved_____
_____
_____
_____

Weary_____
_____
_____
_____

Cold_____
_____
_____

Disinterested_____
_____
_____
_____

WORKBOOK SECTION
Identify Your Feelings

Identify Your Feelings And After You've Pinpointed Your True Feelings, Write Down Why You Believe You Feel This Way And What You Think Can Be Done To Resolve Your Issues...

Identify Your Feelings (How Do You Feel)	Why Do You Feel This Way - What Do You Think You Can Do To Resolve Your Issues Or What Would You Like Someone To Do For You...

Identify Your Feelings (How Do You Feel)	Why Do You Feel This Way - What Do You Think You Can Do To Resolve Your Issues Or What Would You Like Someone To Do For You...

Identify Your Feelings (How Do You Feel)	Why Do You Feel This Way - What Do You Think You Can Do To Resolve Your Issues Or What Would You Like Someone To Do For You...

Identify Your Feelings (How Do You Feel)	Why Do You Feel This Way - What Do You Think You Can Do To Resolve Your Issues Or What Would You Like Someone To Do For You...

Identify Your Feelings (How Do You Feel)	Why Do You Feel This Way - What Do You Think You Can Do To Resolve Your Issues Or What Would You Like Someone To Do For You...

Below Is A List Of Affirmations, After You've Identified Your Feelings, Identify Who You Are With Positive Affirmations

1. I Am Different
2. I Am Rare
3. I Am Strong
4. I Have Courage
5. I Am Whole
6. I Am Confident
7. I Am Extraordinary
8. I Am Particular
9. I Am Exclusive
10. I Am Responsible
11. I Am Deserving Of Good Things
12. I Am A Champion At What I Do
13. I Am One Of A Kind
14. I Am Determined To Succeed
15. I Am Not A Quitter
16. I Am Not A Complainer
17. I Am Assertive
18. I Am Self-Reliant
19. I Am Poised
20. I Am Balanced

21. I Am Mentally Healthy
22. I Am Phenomenal
23. I Am Warm Hearted
24. I Am Good-Natured
25. I Am Caring
26. I Am Happy
27. I Am Polite
28. I Am Concerned About Others
29. I Enjoy Myself
30. I Am Gentle
31. I Am Thoughtful
32. I Have New Ideas
33. I Forgive Easily
34. I Always Reach My Goals
35. I Accept
36. I Get Better And Better Every Day
37. I See The Beauty In Everything
38. I Enjoy Discovering New Things
39. I Am In Charge Of My Life
40. I Love People For Who They Are
41. I Maintain Positive Thoughts
42. I Am A Good Friend To My Friends
43. I Am Trustworthy
44. I Am Honest
45. I Know How To Endure
46. I Am Persistent
47. I Am Clear Headed
48. I Am Creative
49. I Believe In Myself
50. I Am Very Helpful

51. I Am A Leader
52. I Am A Good Listener
53. I Am A Giver
54. I Believe In Others
55. I Am Creative
56. I Am A Positive Thinker
57. I'm Optimistic
58. I Am A Problem Solver
59. I Always Look For Resolutions
60. I Do What I Say I'm Going To Do
61. I'm Grateful For Everything
62. I Am Proactive
63. I Excel At What I Do
64. I'm Never Negative
65. I Am Awesome
66. I Have Something To Contribute To The World
67. I Am Bright
68. I Am Resilient
69. I Am A Trailblazer
70. I Am Courageous
71. I Take Pride In My Life
72. I Look For The Good In People
73. I Trust My Heart
74. I Trust God
75. I Believe In God
76. I Love Being Happy
77. I Love To Make Others Smile
78. I Love Helping People
79. I Love Supporting People

80. I Am Stable
81. I Am Full Of Ideas
82. I Love Knowledge
83. I Enjoy Learning
84. I Am A Peacemaker
85. I Am Proud Of Who I Am
86. I Am Successful At What I Do
87. I Enjoy New Opportunities
88. I Am A Winner
89. I Am A Conqueror
90. I Am Confident In What I Do
91. I Am Patient
92. I Am Understanding
93. I Always Reach For The Stars
94. I See Potential In Others
95. I Love Encouraging People
96. I Am Inspirational
97. I Am Important
98. I Matter
99. I Believe In My Dreams
100. I Love The Way I Look
101. I Am Loved By God

WORKBOOK SECTION

Use This Space To Create Your Own Affirmations About Yourself

Use "I Am" Then Add Your Affirmation Behind It

Example: I Am, <u>Worthy</u>

1. I

   AM_____

2. I

   AM_____

3. I

   AM_____

4. I

   AM_____

5. I

   AM_____

6. I

   AM_____

7. I

   AM_____

8. I

   AM_____

9. I

   AM_____

10.   I

   AM_____

11. I

   AM_____

12.   I

   AM_____

13.   I

   AM_____

14.   I

   AM_____

15.   I

    AM_____

16.   I

    AM_____

17.   I

    AM_____

18.   I

    AM_____

19.   I

    AM_____

20.   I

    AM_____

21. I

AM_____

22. I

AM_____

23. I

AM_____

24. I

AM_____

25. I

AM_____

26. I

AM_____

27. I

AM_____

28. I

AM_____

29. I

AM_____

30. I

AM_____

31. I

AM_____

32. I

AM_____

33. I

AM_____

34. I

AM_____

35. I

AM_____

36. I

AM_____

37. I

AM_____

38. I

AM_____

39. I

AM_____

40. I

AM_____

41. I

AM_____

42. I

AM_____

43. I

AM_____

44. I

AM_____

45. I

AM_____

46. I

AM_____

47. I

AM_____

48. I

AM_____

49. I

AM_____

50. I

AM_____

51. I

AM_____

52. I

AM_____

53. I

AM_____

54. I

AM_____

55. I

AM_____

56. I

AM_____

57. I

   AM_____

58. I

   AM_____

59. I

   AM_____

60. I

   AM_____

61. I

   AM_____

62. I

   AM_____

63.   I

   AM_____

64.   I

   AM_____

65.   I

   AM_____

66.   I

   AM_____

67.   I

   AM_____

68.   I

   AM_____

69. I

AM_____

70. I

AM_____

71. I

AM_____

72. I

AM_____

73. I

AM_____

74. I

AM_____

75.   I

   AM_____

76.   I

   AM_____

77.   I

   AM_____

78.   I

   AM_____

79.   I

   AM_____

80.   I

   AM_____

81. I

AM_____

82. I

AM_____

83. I

AM_____

84. I

AM_____

85. I

AM_____

86. I

AM_____

87. I

AM_____

88. I

AM_____

89. I

AM_____

90. I

AM_____

91. I

AM_____

92. I

AM_____

93. I

AM_____

94. I

AM_____

95. I

AM_____

96. I

AM_____

97. I

AM_____

98. I

AM_____

99.   I

   AM_____

100.   I

   AM_____

Use This 30 Day Space To Journal Your Journey To Loving And Becoming A Better You

On Today,
(date)_____,
I Was Better
Because:_____

_____

_____

_____

_____

_____

_____

_____

On Today,
(date)_____,
I Was Better
Because:_____

_____
_____
_____
_____
_____
_____
_____
_____
_____
_____
_____
_____
_____

On Today,
(date)_____,
I Was Better
Because:_____

_____
_____
_____
_____
_____
_____
_____
_____
_____
_____
_____
_____

On Today,
(date)_____,
I Was Better
Because:_____

_____
_____
_____
_____
_____
_____
_____
_____
_____
_____
_____
_____
_____
_____

On Today,
(date)_____,
I Was Better
Because:_____

_____
_____
_____
_____
_____
_____
_____
_____
_____
_____
_____
_____

On Today,
(date)_____,
I Was Better
Because:_____

_____
_____
_____
_____
_____
_____
_____
_____
_____
_____
_____
_____

On Today,
(date)_____,
I Was Better
Because:_____

_____
_____
_____
_____
_____
_____
_____
_____
_____
_____
_____
_____

On Today,
(date)_____,
I Was Better
Because:_____

_____
_____
_____
_____
_____
_____
_____
_____
_____
_____
_____
_____

On Today,
(date)_____,
I Was Better
Because:_____

_____
_____
_____
_____
_____
_____
_____
_____
_____
_____
_____
_____
_____

On Today,
(date)_____,
I Was Better
Because:_____

_____
_____
_____
_____
_____
_____
_____
_____
_____
_____
_____
_____

On Today,
(date)_____,
I Was Better
Because:_____

_____
_____
_____
_____
_____
_____
_____
_____
_____
_____
_____
_____

On Today,
(date)_____,
I Was Better
Because:_____

_____
_____
_____
_____
_____
_____
_____
_____
_____
_____
_____
_____
_____

On Today,
(date)_____,
I Was Better
Because:_____

_____
_____
_____
_____
_____
_____
_____
_____
_____
_____
_____

On Today,
(date)_____,
I Was Better
Because:_____

_____
_____
_____
_____
_____
_____
_____
_____
_____
_____
_____
_____
_____

On Today,
(date)_____,
I Was Better
Because:_____

_____
_____
_____
_____
_____
_____
_____
_____
_____
_____
_____
_____

On Today,
(date)_____,
I Was Better
Because:_____

_____
_____
_____
_____
_____
_____
_____
_____
_____
_____
_____

On Today,
(date)_____,
I Was Better
Because:_____

_____
_____
_____
_____
_____
_____
_____
_____
_____
_____
_____
_____
_____

On Today,
(date)_____,
I Was Better
Because:_____
_____
_____
_____
_____
_____
_____
_____
_____
_____
_____
_____

On Today,
(date)_____,
I Was Better
Because:_____
_____
_____
_____
_____
_____
_____
_____
_____
_____
_____
_____
_____

On Today,
(date)_____,
I Was Better
Because:_____

_____
_____
_____
_____
_____
_____
_____
_____
_____
_____
_____
_____

On Today,
(date)_____,
I Was Better
Because:_____

_____
_____
_____
_____
_____
_____
_____
_____
_____
_____
_____
_____

On Today,
(date)_____,
I Was Better
Because:_____

_____
_____
_____
_____
_____
_____
_____
_____
_____
_____
_____
_____

On Today,
(date)_____,
I Was Better
Because:_____

_____
_____
_____
_____
_____
_____
_____
_____
_____
_____
_____
_____
_____

On Today,
(date)_____,
I Was Better
Because:_____

_____
_____
_____
_____
_____
_____
_____
_____
_____
_____
_____
_____

On Today,
(date)_____,
I Was Better
Because:_____

_____
_____
_____
_____
_____
_____
_____
_____
_____
_____
_____
_____

On Today,
(date)_____,
I Was Better
Because:_____

_____
_____
_____
_____
_____
_____
_____
_____
_____
_____
_____
_____

On Today,
(date)_____,
I Was Better
Because:_____

_____
_____
_____
_____
_____
_____
_____
_____
_____
_____
_____
_____
_____

On Today,
(date)_____,
I Was Better
Because:_____

_____

_____

_____

_____

_____

_____

_____

_____

_____

_____

_____

_____

On Today,
(date)_____,
I Was Better
Because:_____

_____
_____
_____
_____
_____
_____
_____
_____
_____
_____
_____
_____

On Today,
(date)_____,
I Was Better
Because:_____

_____
_____
_____
_____
_____
_____
_____
_____
_____
_____
_____

SAVE MY LIFE
PANIC REPORT SHEETS

(Check Off What Applies To You AND Rip One Of These Sheets Out As You Need It And Turn It In To Your Teacher, Counselor, Principal, Friend, Parent Or Neighbor)

My Name Is:_____
Date:_____
I'm Being Bullied_____
I'm Being Taunted_____
I'm Being Talked About_____
I'm Being Intimidated_____
I'm Being Beat Up_____
I'm Being Ignored_____
I'm Being Cast Out_____
I'm Being Looked Over_____
I'm Being Picked On_____
I'm Being Laughed At_____
I'm Being Inappropriately Touched_____
I'm Being Molested_____
I'm Being Mistreated_____

*** Fill In Your Own

I'm Being_____
_____
_____

SAVE MY LIFE

PANIC REPORT SHEETS

(Check Off What Applies To You AND Rip One Of These Sheets Out As You Need It And Turn It In To Your Teacher, Counselor, Principal, Friend, Parent Or Neighbor)

My Name Is:_____
Date:_____
I'm Being Bullied_____
I'm Being Taunted_____
I'm Being Talked About_____
I'm Being Intimidated_____
I'm Being Beat Up_____
I'm Being Ignored_____
I'm Being Cast Out_____
I'm Being Looked Over_____
I'm Being Picked On_____
I'm Being Laughed At_____
I'm Being Inappropriately Touched_____
I'm Being Molested_____
I'm Being Mistreated_____
*** Fill In Your Own
I'm Being_____
_____
_____

SAVE MY LIFE PANIC REPORT SHEETS

(Check Off What Applies To You AND Rip One Of These Sheets Out As You Need It And Turn It In To Your Teacher, Counselor, Principal, Friend, Parent Or Neighbor)

My Name Is:_____
Date:_____
I'm Being Bullied_____
I'm Being Taunted_____
I'm Being Talked About_____
I'm Being Intimidated_____
I'm Being Beat Up_____
I'm Being Ignored_____
I'm Being Cast Out_____
I'm Being Looked Over_____
I'm Being Picked On_____
I'm Being Laughed At_____
I'm Being Inappropriately Touched_____
I'm Being Molested_____
I'm Being Mistreated_____

*** Fill In Your Own
I'm Being_____
_____
_____

SAVE MY LIFE
PANIC REPORT SHEETS

(Check Off What Applies To You AND Rip One Of These Sheets Out As You Need It And Turn It In To Your Teacher, Counselor, Principal, Friend, Parent Or Neighbor)

My Name Is:_____
Date:_____
I'm Being Bullied_____
I'm Being Taunted_____
I'm Being Talked About_____
I'm Being Intimidated_____
I'm Being Beat Up_____
I'm Being Ignored_____
I'm Being Cast Out_____
I'm Being Looked Over_____
I'm Being Picked On_____
I'm Being Laughed At_____
I'm Being Inappropriately Touched_____
I'm Being Molested_____
I'm Being Mistreated_____

*** Fill In Your Own

I'm Being_____
_____
_____

SAVE MY LIFE

PANIC REPORT SHEETS

(Check Off What Applies To You AND Rip One Of These Sheets Out As You Need It And Turn It In To Your Teacher, Counselor, Principal, Friend, Parent Or Neighbor)

My Name Is:_____
Date:_____
I'm Being Bullied_____
I'm Being Taunted_____
I'm Being Talked About_____
I'm Being Intimidated_____
I'm Being Beat Up_____
I'm Being Ignored_____
I'm Being Cast Out_____
I'm Being Looked Over_____
I'm Being Picked On_____
I'm Being Laughed At_____
I'm Being Inappropriately Touched_____
I'm Being Molested_____
I'm Being Mistreated_____

*** Fill In Your Own

I'm Being_____
_____
_____

SAVE MY LIFE

PANIC REPORT SHEETS

(Check Off What Applies To You AND Rip One Of These Sheets Out As You Need It And Turn It In To Your Teacher, Counselor, Principal, Friend, Parent Or Neighbor)

My Name Is:_____
Date:_____
I'm Being Bullied_____
I'm Being Taunted_____
I'm Being Talked About_____
I'm Being Intimidated_____
I'm Being Beat Up_____
I'm Being Ignored_____
I'm Being Cast Out_____
I'm Being Looked Over_____
I'm Being Picked On_____
I'm Being Laughed At_____
I'm Being Inappropriately Touched_____
I'm Being Molested_____
I'm Being Mistreated_____

*** Fill In Your Own

I'm
Being_____
_____
_____

SAVE MY LIFE

PANIC REPORT SHEETS

(Check Off What Applies To You AND Rip One Of These Sheets Out As You Need It And Turn It In To Your Teacher, Counselor, Principal, Friend, Parent Or Neighbor)

My Name Is:_____
Date:_____
I'm Being Bullied_____
I'm Being Taunted_____
I'm Being Talked About_____
I'm Being Intimidated_____
I'm Being Beat Up_____
I'm Being Ignored_____
I'm Being Cast Out_____
I'm Being Looked Over_____
I'm Being Picked On_____
I'm Being Laughed At_____
I'm Being Inappropriately Touched_____
I'm Being Molested_____
I'm Being Mistreated_____

*** Fill In Your Own

I'm Being_____
_____
_____

Save My Life Suspicion Sheet

Date:_____

I Believe We Could Be In Danger Because,

Suspicion:_____

_____
_____
_____
_____
_____
_____
_____
_____
_____
_____
_____

Share Your Experiences Good Or Bad And Learn How To Ask Questions

It's Good To Share Your Experiences. I Tell People Sharing Your Experiences Good Or Bad Will Help You Grow. When You Share Your Experiences With People, You Help Them:

- Achieve
- Feel Accepted
- Feel Comfortable And At Ease
- You Also Make People Feel There's Someone Else That Understands What They're Going Through.

Sharing Your Experiences Helps Other Students Open Up. Most Of The Time Students Will Share What They're Going Through, When They Can Relate To Someone Else's Story. In Many Cases, Sharing Stories Are Therapeutic And Hence Helps Others To Overcome.

Never Be Ashamed To Share Your Experiences Good Or Bad, You May Just Help Save Someone's Life.

Subject: Fw: Response to Your Message
From: Pamela Denise Brown (pamelainthelight@yahoo.com)
To: booksspeakforyou@yahoo.com;
Date: Monday, May 16, 2016 9:06 PM

---- Forwarded Message ----

From: The White House <noreply@whitehouse.gov>
To: "pamelainthelight@yahoo.com" <pamelainthelight@yahoo.com>
Sent: Monday, April 25, 2016 3:15 PM
Subject: Response to Your Message

THE WHITE HOUSE
WASHINGTON

Dear Pamela:

Thank you for writing, and for your service as an educator. I want to thank you for your tireless efforts to lift up our next generation of thinkers, dreamers, and doers.

American educators shoulder the great responsibility of preparing young minds for the world they will inherit. I know I wouldn't be where I am today if not for teachers who challenged and pushed me, who put up with and inspired me—who made me feel like I had something to offer, and saw things in me before I saw them in myself. Educators like you are laying the foundation for our future by recognizing the limitless potential in every young person. As you foster your students' growth and vest them with the skills and knowledge they will need to reach for their highest aspirations, you're making a lasting impact not only on the lives of your students, but on the course our country will take.

Please know I'm grateful for all you do, and I wish you the very best.

Sincerely,
Barack Obama

WWW.WHITEHOUSE.GOV

School Book Giveaway Sponsors

1. Pamela Denise Brown Books.com
2. Pamela Denise Brown.com
3. Carrynn's Creations – A Shortcut To Perfection
4. Books Speak For You
5. The Winning Hand Credit Repair.com
6. Bountiful Greeting Cards
7. Treasures Healing Journals.com
8. Write The Prophecy
9. Incorporated By Me.com
10. Expression Coffee Mugs And T-Shirts
11. A New Way
12. Halo Babies Enterprises.com
13. Author And Business Media
14. PDB Enterprises
15. Coleman & Associates, Legal Team

IF YOU Would Like Your Name On This List By Sponsoring A Book Give Away,

Please Contact

Books Speak For You

Or Pamela Denise Brown Books @ 267-318-8933

www.pameladenisebrown.com

Thank You

For Purchasing This Book In Your Purchase, You Are Celebrating With Me The Completion Of One Of God's Many Works Through Me.

Pamela Denise Brown

Contact Information
Website:
www.pameladenisebrown.com
OR
267-318-8933
@Booksspeakforu (twitter)

Email:
Booksspeakforyou@yahoo.com
FaceBook
@pameladenisebrown'sbooksandthings

Special

Dedication To
ALL THE CHILDREN WITH LOVE IN COUNTRIES AROUND THE WORLD

- A

- Afghanistan
- Albania
- Algeria
- Andorra
- Angola
- Antigua and Barbuda
- Argentina
- Armenia
- Australia
- Austria
- Azerbaijan
- B
- Bahamas
- Bahrain
- Bangladesh
- Barbados
- Belarus
- Belgium
- Belize
- Benin
- Bhutan
- Bolivia
- Bosnia and Hiszegovina
- Botswana
- Brazil
- Brunei
- Bulgaria
- Burkina Faso
- Burundi
- C
- Cabo Verde
- Cambodia
- Cameroon
- Canada
- Central African Republic (CAR)
- Chad
- Chile
- China
- Colombia
- Comoros
- Democratic Republic of the Congo
- Republic of the Congo
- Costa Rica
- Cote d'Ivoire
- Croatia
- Cuba
- Cyprus
- Czech Republic
- D
- Denmark
- Djibouti

- Dominica
- Dominican Republic
- E
- Ecuador
- Egypt
- El Salvador
- Equatorial Guinea
- Eritrea
- Estonia
- Ethiopia
- F
- Fiji
- Finland
- France
- G
- Gabon
- Gambia
- Georgia
- Germany
- Ghana
- Greece
- Grenada
- Guatemala
- Guinea
- Guinea-Bissau
- Guyana
- H
- Haiti
- Honduras
- Hungary
- I
- Iceland
- India
- Indonesia
- Iran
- Iraq
- Ireland
- Israel
- Italy
- J
- Jamaica
- Japan
- Jordan
- K
- Kazakhstan
- Kenya
- Kiribati
- Kosovo
- Kuwait
- Kyrgyzstan
- L
- Laos
- Latvia
- Lebanon
- Lesotho

- Liberia
- Libya
- Liechtenstein
- Lithuania
- Luxembourg
- M
- Macedonia
- Madagascar
- Malawi
- Malaysia
- Maldives
- Mali
- Malta
- Marshall Islands
- Mauritania
- Mauritius
- Mexico
- Micronesia
- Moldova
- Monaco
- Mongolia
- Montenegro
- Morocco
- Mozambique
- Myanmar (Burma)
- N
- Namibia

- Nauru
- Nepal
- Nethislands
- New Zealand
- Nicaragua
- Niger
- Nigeria
- North Korea
- Norway
- O
- Oman
- P
- Pakistan
- Palau
- Palestine
- Panama
- Papua New Guinea
- Paraguay
- Peru
- Philippines
- Poland
- Portugal

- Q
- Qatar
- R
- Romania
- Russia

- Rwanda
- S
- St. Kitts and Nevis
- St. Lucia
- St. Vincent and the Grenadines
- Samoa
- San Marino
- Sao Tome and Principe
- Saudi Arabia
- Senegal
- Serbia
- Seychelles
- Sierra Leone
- Singapore
- Slovakia
- Slovenia
- Solomon Islands
- Somalia
- South Africa
- South Korea
- South Sudan
- Spain
- Sri Lanka
- Sudan
- Suriname
- Swaziland
- Sweden
- Switzerland
- Syria
- T
- Taiwan
- Tajikistan
- Tanzania
- Thailand
- Timor-Leste
- Togo
- Tonga
- Trinidad and Tobago
- Tunisia
- Turkey
- Turkmenistan
- Tuvalu
- U
- Uganda
- Ukraine
- United Arab Emirates (UAE)
- United Kingdom (UK)
- United States of America (USA)
- Uruguay

- Uzbekistan
- V
- Vanuatu
- Vatican City (Holy See)
- Venezuela
- Vietnam
- Y
- Yemen
- Z
- Zambia
- Zimbabwe

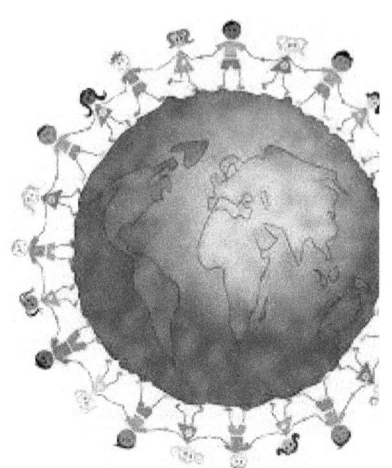

ANOTHER SPECIAL
DEDICATION TO ALL THE
CHILDREN WITH LOVE
IN CITIES IN THE
UNITED STATES OF
AMERICA

Albany, NY
Albuquerque, NM
Anchorage, AK
Annapolis, MD
Atlanta, GA
Atlantic City, NJ
Augusta, ME
Austin, TX
Bakersfield, CA
Baltimore, MD
Baton Rouge, LA
Billings, MT
Biloxi, MS
Bismarck, ND
Bloomsburg, PA
Boise, ID
Boston, MA
Buffalo, NY
Burlington, VT
Carson City, NV
Charleston, SC
Charleston, WV
Charlotte, NC
Charlottesville, VA
Cheyenne, WY
Chicago, IL
Chicago, IL
Cleveland, OH
Colorado Springs, CO
Columbia, SC
Columbus, OH
Concord, CA
Concord, NH
Corpus Christi, TX
Dallas, TX
Davenport, IA
Daytona, FL
Denver, CO
Des Moines, IA
Des Plaines, IL
Detroit, MI
Dover, DE

Durham, NC
Erie, PA
Eugene, OR
Fayetteville, NC
Flagstaff, AZ
Frankfort, KY
Ft. Lauderdale, FL
Gettysburg, PA
Greenville, SC
Hampton Roads, VA
Harrisburg, PA
Hartford, CT
Helena, MT
Hollywood, CA
Honolulu, HI
Houston, TX
Huntsville, AL
Indianapolis, IN
Jackson, MS
Jackson Hole-Grand Tetons, WY
Jacksonville, FL
Jefferson City, MO
Jim Thorpe, PA
Juneau, AK
Kansas City, MO
Knoxville, TN
Lake Tahoe, NV
Lancaster, PA
Lancaster / Central PA
Lansing, MI
Las Vegas, NV
Las Vegas, NV
Lexington, KY
Lincoln, NE
Little Rock, AR
Long Island, NY
Los Angeles, CA
Los Angeles, CA
Louisville, KY
Madison, WI
Manchester, NH
Maryville, TN
Memphis, TN
Miami, FL
Miami, FL
Milwaukee, WI
Minneapolis, MN
Mobile, AL
Montgomery, AL
Montpelier, VT
Morrison, IL
Nashville, TN
New Haven, CT
New Orleans, LA
New York: Bronx
New York: Brooklyn

New York: Manhattan
New York: Queens
New York City
Newark, NJ
Niagara Falls, NY
Northville, MI
Oklahoma City, OK
Orlando, FL
Olympia, WA
Omaha, NE
Orange County, CA
Palm Springs, CA
Pensacola, FL
Philadelphia, PA
Phoenix, AZ
Pierre, SD
Pittsburgh, PA
Portland, ME
Portland, OR
Providence, RI
Pueblo, CO
Raleigh, NC
Rapid City, SD
Reno, NV
Richmond, VA
Sacramento, CA
Salt Lake City, UT
San Diego, CA
San Francisco, CA
Santa Cruz, CA
Santa Fe, NM
Scranton, PA
Seattle, WA
Sedona, AZ
Shreveport, LA
Silicon Valley, CA
Springfield, IL
St. Joseph, MO
St. Paul, MN
St. Louis, MO
State College, PA
SurfScranton, PA
Syracuse, NY
Tacoma, WA
Tallahassee, FL
Tampa, FL
Topeka, KS
Trenton, NJ
Tulsa, OK
Tuscon, AZ
Tyler, TX
Washington, DC
Wichita, KS
Wilkes-Barre, PA
Williamsburg, VA
Williamsport, PA

Wilmington, DE
Yuma, AZ